DESIGNED TO GO THE DISTANCE

A Survival Guide for the Creative Professional

FIRST EDITION

by

MITCH DOWELL

Copyright © 2016 by Mitch Dowell. All rights reserved.

Published in the USA

ISBN-13: 978-1540537614

ISBN-10: 1540537617

No part of this book may be reproduced in any form unless written permission is granted from the author or publisher. No electronic reproductions, information storage, or retrieval systems may be used or applied to any part of this book without written permission.

Due to the variable conditions, materials, and individual skills, the publisher, author, editor, translator, transcriber, and/or designer disclaim any liability for loss or injury resulting from the use or interpretation of any information presented in this publication. No liability is assumed for damages resulting from the use of the information contained herein.

Acknowledgements

I would like to thank and acknowledge the following people for their indirect influence on this book. First, my wife Meredith, who is married to this career creative and I really don't know how she does it (or how *any* spouse married to a career creative does it, really). Every boss over the years who took a chance on me, but specifically E. Frank Wade for giving me my first "real" career break, Ron Ball for recognizing the value of creativity and allowing me to fill that void, J. Michael Myshrall for just letting me do my thing and putting in a few good words for me over the years, and Jessica Feltz for referring more clients than one could possibly comprehend. And most indirectly, Susan M. Brackney for paying it forward years ago to the highly creative, lost (and not-so-lost) souls out there. Lastly, to all of those who have bet against me in one way or another, thank you for unknowingly fueling a competitive and respectable career (and yes, I know you're not done with me yet). And to the many other influencers not mentioned here by name, you know who you are. Thank you.

CONTENTS

Introduction 1

Square Pegs in a World of Round Holes 5

Introverts, Extroverts, and Creativity 11

Getting Comfortable With Risk 19

The Inconvenient Nature of Creativity 25

Establishing a Philosophy 31

Bridging The Creative Divide 35

Your Obligation to Non-Conformity 39

The Emotional Intelligence Advantage 43

The Benefits of Boundaries 49

Understanding Comfort Zones 52

Understanding Burnout 59

Balancing Career and Life 67

Handling Criticism Like a Pro 71

When Side Projects Just Make Sense 75

Depression and The Creative Pro 79

The Final Word: Paying it Forward 85

Introduction

This book isn't about creativity. Chances are that you're already a creative professional or you wouldn't have picked up this book. Creatives early in their careers generally aren't concerned about "survival" guides, but those who have been in the field for some time most likely understand that the demands and expectations of their field can take a unique toll on creative professionals. There are many hard lessons that creative professionals must learn that formal education tends to leave out of textbooks. If only there were a book that covered many of the "gotchas", "booby traps" and "landmines" that creative professionals will likely have to navigate through as they pursue their true passions.

Now, I'm not going to tell you that you've just found that book. Such a book would have to fall from the heavens to accurately and completely capture all the topics and scenarios that creative professionals are likely get tripped up by. I'm not sure such a book will ever exist. But hopefully this book provides a good start, and can inspire others to keep the conversation going.

This book also isn't about a specific job or professional role in the creative world, as it will cover topics that can certainly be relevant to many. But you might occasionally notice a slight slant towards the visual arts or scenarios that may favor those in corporate or creative agency careers. As a point of reference, I have been involved in visual branding and graphic design for over 20 years. I have worked on the corporate side of the fence as well as on the agency side. I have spent most of my career in the trenches doing hands-on design and creative work myself, but have also worked in environments where I have managed other creative professionals – both in-house as well as outsourced talent. I have owned my own creative firm, served on non-profit boards, and have been featured in the media for my creative contributions to the business world – all having never set foot inside a college or university classroom – in true, gritty, chip-on-the-shoulder, underdog fashion.

Although I'm humbled by these achievements, nothing has been more humbling than learning many things in my creative career the hard way. Having said that, this book isn't about providing any shortcuts to creative career fulfillment either. There are no shortcuts that I am aware of. That is not how we learn best or accumulate our most rewarding experiences anyway.

2   *Designed to Go the Distance*

So then, is this a "motivational book" for the creative professional? Not necessarily. But I do hope that the perspectives captured in these pages are inspiring. Think of this book more as a late-night barstool or coffeehouse conversation between two creatives. A creative "pep talk" so-to-speak. And just like any pep talk in life, the objective in these pages is more to provide food-for-thought, rather than proven, actionable advice that will apply to everyone.

Also, if you're holding this book in your hands, or have peeked ahead at the total page count, you've probably noticed something else. We're not dealing with a novel here. This can be a quick, weekend-read – or for some of the faster readers out there, you can probably knock this book out on a typical cross-country flight (flight delays and layovers included). Some of the best "pep talks" get to the point. They are not drawn out life lessons that take forever to get through. If you have a short-attention span like me, you know we don't have time for that kind of read.

Because this is more of a quick, straight-talk read, I'm not going to fluff up the pages with a bunch of creative doodles and illustrations to feed your creative soul while you read. Maybe in a future edition.

So, with that understanding, grab a cup of coffee or your favorite beverage, and maybe even a highlighter - or even better - a pencil to jot down some thoughts (there's a Notes section in the back), and let's dive in and talk about what it might take to create and maintain a fulfilling creative career – one that is *designed to go the distance.*

1

Square Pegs in a World of Round Holes

Meryl Steep said it best, "what makes you different or weird – that's your strength.[1]" If you fail to remember anything from this book, please remember that. Chances are that your entire creative career will revolve around that theory. It will be both a blessing and a curse throughout your career, but it will be worth it every step of the way.

Let's think a minute about what the word "creative" implies. By definition, it means "resulting from originality of thought, expression, etc.; imaginative.[2]" There are three key words to focus on in that definition: *originality, expression* and *imaginative* - so let's break it down.

Originality implies a first-of-a-kind – something that has never previously existed. *Expression* is an "indication of feeling, spirit, character, etc., as on the face, in the voice, or in artistic execution.[3]" *Imaginative* is a word related to "forming mental images or concepts of what is not actually present to the senses.[4]"

Creative personalities simply think differently. That's the whole point. That is the blessing in it all – it's the value that creatives bring to the world, as well as leave behind in their legacies.

The moment that you identify your creativity as the largest value that you can contribute to the world is a beautiful thing. Many people go through their entire lives never identifying that one thing that really makes them tick. And furthermore, to have the opportunity to build a career around that is a truly wonderful thing.

On the other hand, there are many creatives who don't see themselves as necessarily "creative." They just "are who they are." They've always been "that way", whatever that means. For example, although many of my peers and colleagues throughout the years

6   *Designed to Go the Distance*

have referred to me as "creative" – and I always took it as a compliment – it wasn't until about 20 years into my career that I "gave in" to the word and embraced it as something that perhaps set me apart from others.

That is the "blessing" of it all. But there is also a "curse" on the flipside as well. Perhaps curse is a rather extreme word to use to refer to it, but if you've been a creative professional for many years, you might understand what I'm referring to.

When we consider the names of major innovators in modern history, some names that come to mind might include the likes of Steve Jobs, Henry Ford, Thomas Edison, Albert Einstein and many others. In terms of impactful creatives in pop culture, perhaps the names may include Bob Dylan, Prince, Michael Jackson, Robin Williams and Woody Allen to name a few. The lists go on and on. We idolize these individuals for the end results of their work and for the impact they may have made on our lives, and we put them on a pedestal for what they have shown us on the surface through their creative accomplishments.

What we don't see on the surface, however, is the blood, sweat and tears that went into it all. We don't see the sacrifices that these individuals had to make to bring their art to the surface - sacrifices that may include failed relationships, depression, alcohol or drug

Mitch Dowell   7

abuse, or other unfortunate experiences that may have been part of their success story.

Or maybe you do. After all, we all love a good "Rocky" story. But let me repeat that entire paragraph, changing only one word..

"What we don't *feel* on the surface, however, is the blood, sweat and tears that went into it all. We don't *feel* the sacrifices that these individuals had to make to bring their art to the surface - sacrifices that may include failed relationships, depression, alcohol or drug abuse, or other unfortunate experiences that may have been part of their success story."

This is the "curse" that I am referring to, and a topic that I will dive into much deeper later in this book. But for now, let's just say that creative professionals are highly emotional creatures who arguably put more on the line – *emotionally*, and at a higher level of sustained intensity, than compared to those in non-creative career fields. And yet, you may never know exactly how much because it won't often be seen on the surface. This even applies to the most introverted creative professionals as well.

This is where the "Square Pegs in a World of Round Holes" reality comes in. There is a certain cultural divide that exists in the business world between those who lead a highly creative career existence vs. those who perhaps don't. Thus, there is a constant, undercurrent of friction that exists in the boardrooms, the cubicles and in the lunch

8 *Designed to Go the Distance*

rooms across the business world. While this very world needs a constant stream of new ideas and new ways of thinking to evolve, survive and thrive - it is also a world that values predictability and aversion to high risk whenever possible.

Where those two realities meet is rarely a comfortable and cushy place. And yet, it's usually the exact place where the value of the creative professional needs to be leveraged the most. It's often an emotionally and intellectually intensive place and one that is not for the faint of heart. Therefore, there is often a certain non-conformist, "misfit" profile that tends to do well in this space. But that doesn't make it any more comfortable or cushy for those individuals. It just happens to be an ideal fertile ground for creativity, and both smart organizations and smart creatives know this.

Simply put, people who stand out often do so because they don't fit in. That is the whole point. Smart creatives know this and embrace it.

So, if you want to stand out in your career or in your life, you must get very comfortable with not fitting in. You are going to have to embrace that constant friction. You are going to have to be comfortable being that square peg in a world of round holes.

Mitch Dowell   9

2

Introverts, Extroverts, and Creativity

The introvert vs. extrovert debate is a never-ending one in our society. The various arguments can range from which demographic is more productive, to which demographic is more likely to live longer. However, the topic invites an interesting and perhaps very relevant conversation specifically regarding creativity.

While absolutely anyone can have a successful and productive creative career – regardless of which personality demographic that they feel they fit into, there seems to be a regular fascination specifically regarding *introverts* and creativity.

There are many scientific (and not-so-scientific) studies on the topic of introversion and creativity, as well as news articles that come to the surface from time-to-time on the latest findings. A simple internet search should bring up plenty of reading material on the topic. While this book is not based on either science or deep academic research - but rather on an author's personal and professional first-hand experience – the discussion on introversion here lies primarily on common sense.

There are three general ways that creativity can be harvested – by oneself, through a collaboration with others, or by a combination of both. Let's explore all three.

Creative professionals who work primarily by themselves (for example graphic designers or authors), primarily have the canvas to themselves – literally and metaphorically. In these scenarios, it's important for the professional to close themselves off to the outside world in order to "get into their zone" and create their magic. With ongoing projects that may span many different clients or creative publications, it's not uncommon for these types of creatives to work

12   *Designed to Go the Distance*

in solitude much of the working year. This can both attract introverts to this style of work, as well as create introverts because of it.

Creativity can also result from a collaboration with others, where an individual may not necessarily have the entire canvas to themselves. Songwriting is a good example. Many songs that we hear over the radio and internet were the collaborative result of everyone in the band, bringing their individual pieces to the canvas to form a whole. These types of creative scenarios can suit both introverts and extroverts quite well.

To describe the combination of both, let's stick with music as an example. All four members of The Beatles were songwriters. However, as you study their catalog of music, you will find examples of both collaborations and individual songs that were written by a sole member.

While the number of paths through creativity and the various player combinations involved can be a never-ending discussion, there are three common factors that are involved in most creative processes: *strategic thinking, problem solving, and originality* – that *collectively* need to make an emotional connection with the target audience.

Let's take graphic design for example. A single, full-page print ad must be *strategic* for positioning both the brand, as well as the product. The print ad must also convey that it *solves a problem* for the target audience. And lastly, the ad must make an *emotional connection* with the target audience through a sense of originality for it to stand out among the numerous other ads and product offerings out there.

We could apply the same example to music. A songwriter must think somewhat strategically in how music and lyrics actually fit together. An orchestra conductor could arguably be considered somewhat of a musical "strategist" with all the parts and pieces that need to fit together. There is also problem solving at play in music, commonly found in lyrics that involve a story and a plot that involves some kind of conflict. And of course, originality lies both at the individual music level, as well as the collective sound of the band.

While these may not be perfect, air-tight examples of the trifecta that often needs to take place in the creative process, I'm confident that most creative professionals reading this will get the gist. For the human brain to deliver strategic thinking, problem solving, and originality – all within the same creation – the demands that the creator dive deep into oneself, or among a small group of others, are quite enormous. Therefore, the environments and conditions under which creators must create often tend to favor the introverted personality style. For example, many graphic designers prefer to work in solitude to get into their zone – or in the very least wear headphones to audibly take them away to where they need to go.

14   *Designed to Go the Distance*

Similarly, many computer programmers and coders often prefer to work under darker lighting in order to concentrate and focus on-screen. Both are examples where again, the creative process and introverted personalities make common sense bed fellows.

All this of course is commonly understood within the creative community, specifically within ad agencies and the like; but not so much within non-creative, corporate environments - and that is commonly where friction often lies, and personalities often clash.

Introverted, in-house creatives in the corporate world tend to have it rough, especially on smaller teams. Marketing tends to be the department where you will find most career creatives, and therefore, most introverted personality types.

Yet marketing also tends to work side-by-side with the Sales department – a department that culturally is less concerned about creativity, and more directly concerned about meeting quotas and chasing the almighty dollar – and naturally, this is where you find a lot of extroverts.

In lies the crossroads of different personality types with different true passions at heart – both forced to salute to the same corporate mission. And this is where things can get unnecessarily messy between creatives and non-creatives, and between introverts and extroverts.

Mitch Dowell   15

While leadership comes in many styles, Corporate America generally has a very stereotypical, cookie-cutter view of leadership that tends to favor extroverts. Visions of the pump-you-up-Tony Robbins-type tend to come to mind, or the wing-tip-wearing, Aqua-Velva®-smelling type of micro-manager that is up and down the hallways in everyone's business.

Leadership styles and philosophies are different with creatives – compared to the "stereotypical" teachings of leadership. Most creatives lead through their body of work. That's the whole point of their existence. Therefore, talk is cheap. And therefore, introversion just makes sense. In many corporate environments, these introverted creative leaders tend to be seen, or at least treated – directly or indirectly, as second-rate – and for no good reason whatsoever.

Your job as a creative professional is to not get caught up in the introvert vs. extrovert bullshit debate. You are who you are, regardless of which personality type you fall under. Creatives need to keep their eye on the ball (the work at hand), while building their professional relationships on their own terms, not under someone else's. Let the friction exist in the air. It can actually be good for you and for the organization you work for.

16   *Designed to Go the Distance*

3

Getting Comfortable With Risk

Risk. You've gotta love it if your job is to push the envelope day in and day out. While the media often publishes articles about the possible connection between risk and creativity, every creative professional or non-conformist knows that – just like peanut butter and jelly - risk and creativity just go together.

Most risk involves an absence of confidence in what the outcome will be, and that absence of confidence can be scary. What you envision the end result will be when you start creating, and what the end results actually turn out to be can be two different things.

Therefore, every creative journey involves the risk of not ending up where you expected to be. What you are left with can be comfortable, or uncomfortable, depending on the outcome.

Chasing a creative idea can be like entering a maze. You may enter with an idea of where it may lead you, but you don't really know for sure. And if you get lost and decide to backtrack, there's a good chance that you may eventually find your way back. But even *that* isn't necessarily certain.

There are some creative processes where backtracking is not even an option. A chef, for example, may have a limited number of ingredients to choose from, a limited time to make the dish, and no pre-planned recipe ahead of time. In other words, he or she has decided to just wing it. But once the ingredients are put into motion, it may not be possible to just start over if things don't go as planned. Starting over may not be an option. And so, the pressure is on, as well as the adrenaline rush that comes with it, and interestingly that can either bring out the best creative work under certain circumstances, or the worst. But regardless of possible "best or worst" outcomes, risk in the very least will always help you push your own self-imposed boundaries.

Charting new territory in the creative process like this, knowingly or unexpectedly, can be scary and unnerving to some. But to most creative professionals, this type of risk is often at the core of most

18 *Designed to Go the Distance*

creative processes. Not only is it not always a bad thing, risk can actually be your best friend in the creative process. The risk of allowing something to just happen, to risk the unknown, can be invigorating to you as a creative professional.

As you find yourself in these moments, you must intuitively know when to go all in and immerse yourself entirely, because in the creative process, "what you are seeking is also seeking you." That intuition will naturally come with time through the experience of accurately listening to and reading your gut feelings.

As a creative professional, you must be comfortable with the uncertainty that creative risk taking brings on, but unsatisfied until you successfully make your way through it. But even successfully making your way through a creative challenge, the risk doesn't end there.

There is also something called "post-creative" risk, also known as the necessity of putting your creative work out into the world, as it makes you vulnerable to criticism from your peers and your competitors. Creatives often risk sticking their necks out and baring their soul publicly. And since no one wants to be responsible for a failed project, a marketplace flop or a PR embarrassment, those who are truly comfortable in their creative skin are often quite comfortable with risk taking, and have a tolerance for the occasional failure that comes with it.

Mitch Dowell   19

The last area of risk worth mentioning does not lie directly within or after the creative process, but instead sometimes around it. For example, some may include the risk of being in way over your head, having too much on your plate, or biting off more than you can chew workwise. This can be a project killer, as well as lead to burnout over time (I discuss burnout in detail elsewhere in this book).

OK, so you get it now, and you're all on board with risk taking and the fact that it just naturally goes together with creativity, right? Great! But wait… there is a potentially dangerous side to the risk-taking mentality that every creative professional needs to be mindful of, and that is the allure of risk outside of one's career.

Yes, that's correct. The allure of risk can sometimes find its way into other areas of a creative's life when he or she is not looking. While risk taking goes with the territory of professional creativity, one should be cautious about risk when it comes to matters such as personal and business finances, relationships, and personal health and wellness, to name a few. While the adrenaline rush can be welcoming in the creative process, it may not be so welcome in other areas of life. Maintain the proper balance by recognizing how risk, and how you react to it, affects the different areas of your life. It is certainly worth keeping an eye on in your bigger life picture.

20   *Designed to Go the Distance*

4

The Inconvenient Nature of Creativity

So, there you are. You're lying in bed in the middle of the night, and suddenly it hits you. That perfect creative idea. Should you get out of bed and chase it down at all costs, or will you trust yourself to remember it in the morning? Or maybe it comes knocking at 4:58PM on a Friday at the office. Do you log off and go home for the weekend as scheduled, or do you fire up the coffeepot and dig in? After all, it could make or break a project, a client, or a career.

There is no perfect answer for how to respond when inconvenient and unscheduled ideas come knocking, but one thing is for certain, they will come knocking when you least expect it and you will be faced with a tough choice. The unexpected arrival of a new idea can be exhilarating and the creative mojo inside oneself will always want to eagerly answer when it comes knocking. But there can be sacrifices involved when deciding to chase down even the simplest of ideas.

Many creative professionals often struggle with issues relating to both personal relationships and personal health, and these inconvenient and unscheduled ideas are a dominating reason why. It's not that creative professionals are workaholics. Although some may indeed be, even those who only work part-time can agree that creativity is not something that can be easily turned on and off like a light switch – even when that is exactly what you're getting paid to do. Creativity instead has its own energy. Sometimes we're able to control it when it comes knocking, while other times *it controls us* during the process. Either way, it's a beautiful thing.

There is something known in the sport of running referred to as the "runner's high." For example, three or four miles into a runner's training, the runner might experience a certain high, when their breathing, their stride, their speed, their mental state – all possible factors involved in the activity seem to be in perfect harmony with one another, to the point where the runner might feel as if their feet aren't even touching the ground. Some call it being "in the zone", some may refer to it in other terms. But many often indeed compare it to a "high."

Creative professionals experience a very similar feeling. There's a rush there. It's a high of sorts. And like getting high, there can be a period of "crashing" afterword, where the creative professional just feels absolutely exhausted. During the most productive and successful careers, this can take a toll on one's personal relationships and overall personal health.

For those who work a strict 9 to 5, or predictable punch-in-and-punch-out work lifestyle outside of a creative career field, you have it relatively easy compared to the creative professional. Although many creative professionals physically work a predictable schedule, the creative mind has no sense of time. Outside of "normal" working hours, it will clock back in whenever it feels like working again. The off-the-clock human part of us can try to shut it down when it unexpectedly turns on, but is that the right thing to do?

There is no perfect answer, and that is the bitch of it all.

I remember when I was growing up watching children's cartoons, there were often metaphors worked into the animations to educate the viewer and communicate certain life lessons. Often when there was a character who was struggling with making a tough decision between right and wrong, there would be an animated angel over one shoulder of the character, and a devil over the other shoulder.

Mitch Dowell   23

The angel often represented good conscience, and the devil often represented temptation. They both would be whispering into the ear of the indecisive character, pleading their individual cases and reasoning for going their way.

This is the dilemma that career creatives face when inconvenient and unscheduled ideas come knocking after hours. The "angel" in this scenario is often the inner voice reminding us of the need for work/life balance, and reminding us that we're off the clock. The "devil" in this scenario is our creative voice saying, "Hey, I've got a great creative idea about your Project A, or Client B! But I need your help smoothing it out before I forget. Drop everything you're doing right now and work with me!"

One thing that creative professionals know first-hand that non-creatives can't always understand or comprehend – is that very devil can actually be an angel in disguise. And it doesn't just fly in and perch on your shoulder whenever YOU want it to. It does it when IT wants to. So when it arrives, you don't necessarily just flick it off and move on to what you were previously doing, just because you are technically off the clock.

Work/life balance is something that most of our society struggles with these days, regardless of career field. We can blame a good portion of it on the advancement of technology and how the lines separating our digital and off-the-grid lives have been blurred. But work/life balance issues that many creative professionals struggle with have little to do with technology, and more about how their creative brains work in the first place.

I doubt that when John Lennon first was hit with the idea for the song "Imagine", that he paused and said, "Nah, I should probably go do the dishes first." Or when George Lucas first had the inspiration for *Stars Wars* or for *Indiana Jones*, that he refused to excuse himself from the dinner table because it would be disruptive to others in that moment. Of course, I'm not knowledgeable about those specific moments of inspiration, I could be totally incorrect. But hopefully you get my point. Great minds work on their own time. The rest of the person attached to that mind must deal with that reality, and sadly so do others in the lives of the creative professional.

We can try little tricks like keeping a notebook or voice recorder on us wherever we go (most smartphones have those capabilities built in anyway), and this may help lessen the inconvenience of creativity striking when in the middle of other obligations. But while this can be a good idea to ensure that we don't lose the initial ideas that pop into our heads, it helps very little in chasing down those ideas any further in the moment.

See that's the thing that is unique about creative ideas – each idea comes with its own sense of energy. For example, no two people

Mitch Dowell   25

will knock on your front door the same way. Some will have a light, quieter knock, while others may pound like a monster. Some may knock once and leave, while others will knock repeatedly and not leave your doorstep until you answer.

Creative personalities always feel the urge to answer. We can't just turn out the lights and pretend we're not home, because the knocking *comes from within us*, not from outside of us.

So, that can be one of the curses of being a creative professional. In reality, there will always be a friction there when those inconvenient and unscheduled ideas come knocking, both within oneself, as well as within the relationships we strive to maintain outside of our creative gigs.

Maintaining work/life balance is very important in the big picture. The creative mind just doesn't make it so easy.

5

Establishing a Philosophy

In both business and in life, as people accumulate successes and failures, it's very natural that a certain philosophy starts to form and come to the surface. It's a natural occurrence whether we intend it to be or not.

As the old saying goes, "if you don't stand for something, you will fall for anything." Establishing a philosophy isn't so much about taking a stand, but rather having something to come home to throughout your career that just feels right. It becomes your source – your center – your north star.

This philosophy concept that I'm referring to isn't only formed and governed by intellect. It is also something that is felt in your bones and in your heart. Remember, creatives are highly emotional creatures. We don't think first in spreadsheets and analytics; we are instead driven by something more powerful within.

Professional sports can provide endless metaphors for both business and for life in general. Philosophy plays an important part in sports. Let's take the NFL draft for example. Some teams in the first round will take the best, most talented and skilled player available – regardless of whether they actually have a need for that role. After all, there is no such thing as too much talent.

Or is there?

Only 14 players in the history of the National Football League have gone from being the first overall pick in a draft to earning election into the Pro Football Hall of Fame[5]. This is proof that talent will only get you so far.

As a creative professional, accumulating and honing your hands-on skills won't be enough. Not only do you need to surround yourself with the right people and right clients, you also need to have a philosophy to build your career around.

28   *Designed to Go the Distance*

Believe in something. Believe in a certain way of doing things. Believe that the unique way that YOU do things makes sense in the big picture. HAVE A BIG PICTURE. Career philosophies provide meaning. They are the glue to everything that you do. When it comes to creativity - where you are getting paid to create solutions and concepts that don't already exist - your unique philosophy must come through in everything you do.

But here is the good news about this topic. Most creatives, and specifically introverted creatives, are philosophers by nature. They are masterful people watchers, they know how to listen, and they know how to absorb the world around them. The Why is equally (if not more) important than the What. That true nature, together with artistic and creative talent, can change the world; or on a lesser scale, change an industry, an organization, or a campaign.

Whether you have already established a personal philosophy in your line of creative work or not, never stop seeking out the Why in everything. Never stop questioning and challenging everything and everybody – not to be a pain the ass to be around, but to learn as much as possible about the creative that you're passionate about. Sometimes having an intense fascination about the Whys can make the Whats quicker to determine and easier to understand.

Lastly, it's important to realize that establishing a philosophy in your creative career shouldn't start and end with your actual creativity or creative output. Business (and life) is about relationships, therefore you should also have a "people philosophy" ingrained in what you do.

In a perfect world, we are surrounded by people who share the same philosophy and speak the same language as we do. But in the creative world, that isn't always the case. We actually may be surrounded by the opposite crowd, where we may be the ONLY person in the process who is thinking in a certain way. But it is that exact friction in our world that can sometimes bring out our best work, and we need to embrace that.

So as you establish your career philosophies specifically in regard to the company you choose to keep, keep a few of the annoying personalities around – not the ones who you would prefer to beat with a baseball bat – but the ones who you know challenge you in a healthy, constructive and productive way. Both your people philosophy and your creative philosophy will gel together and set you up for a healthy and fulfilling creative career.

6

Bridging The Creative Divide

As a creative professional, you have a responsibility and obligation to the field, to communicate well with others who are on the opposite, non-creative side of the fence. They could be your clients, business partners, fellow employees or others who may have no clue whatsoever what actually goes into what you do.

Many creative professionals blow off this responsibility or give it less value in their careers because it can be quite difficult. There is a lack of understanding between both sides and it takes time and effort to bridge that divide.

It's not about playing well with others. What you do isn't play. It's hard, intensive work. But the creative work you do will actually be the easiest part of what you do. Building and maintaining business relationships with others outside of what you do will require a different kind of effort.

The graphic design culture is an interesting case-in-point. I know a lot of graphic designers who can design pixel-perfect creations and are well known among their creative peers for it – but who appear to lack any basic sense of business and communication skills. Many go to art school and learn their craft – *where they are surrounded by others just like them.* They graduate and go into ad agency work – *where they are surrounded by others just like them.* They go to meetups and networking events specific to their craft – *where they are surrounded by others just like them.*

This kind of tribal behavior among creatives is nothing new. It can provide a logical, safe place among others who understand them, but it does nothing to help build their business communication skills outside of their immediate tribe. In-house, corporate-side designers tend to have a *slight* edge in terms of business communication skills, as they are often forced on a more regular basis to build upon those skills. But a *slight* edge it is.

32   *Designed to Go the Distance*

So this is where the creative divide exists in the business world. It has little to do with creativity, but instead, the communication that is involved in the business of creativity.

Creatives and non-creatives need each other to exist. It's a yin and yang thing. However, more often than not, *non-creatives* tend to be more eager to find common ground in the relationship, whereas creatives often take a more standoffish, stiff-arm approach to these relationships.

Sadly, this is one of the many reasons why creatives struggle to move up the various ladders in their careers. They often get stuck in the trenches in their careers – where their art actually happens – and then bitch about why they were passed up for that Creative Director or Art Director job, or why they can't move over and up to a more broader leadership role.

Business is about relationships. Life is about relationships. You can't just hide within your private, safe place of creativity. That will only work for so long. This does not mean that you need to become an extrovert that you are not, or never want to be either. What this DOES mean is that you're going to have to have a sincere desire to educate and create understanding among those who are not "one of you," because once again, creatives and non-creatives need each other to exist. Non-creatives are not the enemy.

Mitch Dowell   33

Recognize the creative divides that exist in your business relationships and put in the effort to bridge those divides. That's not to say you need to reveal the secrets and recipes of how you do what you do, but do your part to make the common ground that needs to exist a happy place for all who need to meet there.

7

Your Obligation to Non-Conformity

By definition, a non-conformist is a person whose behavior or views do not conform to prevailing ideas or practices. Most creatives are non-conformists. That's the point. The sensitive part of it all, however, is that there is a certain stigma associated with that label, specifically in the business world, that we need to be mindful of.

To the average Joe, the term "non-conformist" often tends to conjure up stereotypical images of radically-minded individuals, who are often considered "unreasonable," "unwilling to compromise," and a "pain in the ass to work or live with." Not entirely true. But one thing that IS true is that non-conformists are the ones who actually change the world. History continually proves it.

Steve Jobs, Henry Ford, Thomas Edison, Martin Luther King Jr, Mahatma Ghandi... any of those names ring a bell? How about George Carlin, Princess Diana, Amelia Earhart or Rosa Parks?

OK, now read those lists again, but this time add your name somewhere in the middle. Does it feel right, or feel weird? Your answer to that question really doesn't matter because non-conformists don't have to be household names or make it into the history books. They just have to be themselves doing whatever it is that is true to their heart, and on whatever scale makes sense to them.

But household name or not, one thing that almost all non-conformists have in common is that they take great risk in just being themselves, and by pursuing personal and professional goals around their unconventional perspectives. This is one of the reasons why I devote a separate chapter in this book entirely to the concept of risk.

But here is the tricky part: as a non-conformist, you must learn how to be a productive and successful non-conformist without being an actual asshole. You will have to learn to balance keeping an open mind to other views and opinions, but without giving up what you believe in and staying the course of what you feel is true. Henry

36 *Designed to Go the Distance*

Ford wasn't the chummiest fellow on the planet. Steve Jobs had also been known to be a challenge to work with. It's not easy being the one who needs to think differently, to fight for new ideas, or go against traditional thinking for the better good of the mission at hand. But you will also have to get others to buy into your ideas, and that will be easier said than done.

Learning how to sell ideas to others can be an art in itself. As a non-conformist, you must be willing to accept this artful challenge. To do this, first you must learn how to read others well. If you are an introvert, you might have somewhat of an advantage, as introverts have been known to be expert people watchers and can often accurately read others quite well. They are always listening and watching, often when people think they are not.

But listening and watching won't be enough. You must get good at planting thought-provoking questions in the minds of others. There can be a certain psychological game that will need to be played in selling your non-conforming ideas and viewpoints. But it should be done in a non-confrontational way. In the best scenarios, the thought-provoking pitch excites others and engages others in a meaningful dialogue. That is what every non-conformist needs to strive for.

Sadly, you will often come across others who simply won't budge: folks who are set in their ways – the ones wearing concrete shoes in their comfort zones and who will defend and guard the way things have always been done like a dog guards a bone. That's life. It just goes with the territory of bringing new ideas into the world.

As a creative professional, non-conformity provides a certain friction that will need to constantly exist in your professional life. It may prove to be both healthy and hurtful at times, but it will be a necessary factor in your creative success.

As a creative professional, know that non-conforming ideas can be your strength. You don't have to be that stereotypical radical and unreasonable non-conformist type. But you DO have an obligation to bring new ideas to the surface and to challenge conventional thinking – and not many *conformists* do that.

8

The Emotional Intelligence Advantage

In life, there is IQ, and then there is EQ (or EI) – *emotional intelligence.*

By definition, *emotional intelligence* is "the capability of individuals to recognize their own, and other people's emotions, to discriminate between different feelings and label them appropriately, to use emotional information to guide thinking and behavior.[6]"

One of the most valuable, hidden assets that you will ever possess in your career and in your life, will be your emotional intelligence. This is where not your skills or know-how is of value, but where the emotional wisdom of your inner Yoda or Papa Smurf must come to the surface.

The business world is not all X's and O's. It's not the cold, sterile and emotionless place we like to make it out to be. Quite the opposite, actually. Business is VERY emotional, especially when it comes to the creative process – the changing of minds and challenging old ways of thinking.

Creatives often struggle in this area throughout their careers. We are emotional creatures. We either fly off the handle at the toughest of workplace challenges, or the opposite – we retreat within ourselves. Knowing when, and most importantly, HOW, to stand up and fight for your ideas and challenge the status quo takes not just intuition, but effectively reading both yourself as well as others.

Sometimes there can be valuable intelligence that can come to the surface when team members fly off the handle during intensive creative collaborations. It's in those moments that you truly find out what people stand for (or what they *won't* stand for), how passionate they are about it, and how much they are willing to risk for it. It can be either inspiring, or damaging. Your job as a creative leader is to allow a climate where your creative team feels comfortable enough to "lay it all out there", but also to coach and mentor your team to identify the right scenarios where it is more likely to be inspiring, and not permanently damaging.

The status quo is always a hard nut to crack. It will defend its way of thinking and protect its comfort zones at all costs. The status quo does not like change without its consent and it can be extremely frustrating at times.

Creative professionals are problem solvers. We don't like to sweep issues under the carpet or kick the can down the road. That is not why we exist or why we get hired to do what we do. But sadly, that can very often be the cause of the problems that we inherit and are expected to solve in the first place.

I've had moments earlier in my career where I've yelled at team members, unfairly and publicly challenged my superiors, and even lost my cool in front of clients a couple of times. I've had my share of moments where my emotional intelligence was nowhere to be found. I think we all have had similar moments. When we learn from those situations, we in turn become more emotionally intelligent in our most intensive creative work.

Sometimes the creativity and collaboration process can be like a tug-of-war event. Sometimes there will be grunting, and there will be grit – it may even get dirty and muddy in the middle. Now imagine if you added Yoda or Papa Smurf to the end of your side of the rope.

Mitch Dowell   41

That's where emotional intelligence comes in as a creative leader. You set the tone not only for yourself, but for others pulling in the same direction. You have the opportunity to lead the creative process with a certain appropriate energy that is more likely to provide a successful outcome. Your emotional intelligence will allow you to become not just a better leader of creative processes, but a better leader in general.

All of this is so much easier said than done. Emotional intelligence is difficult because it requires constant, never-ending work. Team players often come and go, and new personalities can come into the mix with different philosophies, perspectives and agendas, which can often change the creative chemistry in the air – sometimes for the better – or sometimes for the worse.

If you are in a creative leadership role, here are some tips that can help you work on your emotional intelligence skills (they are good tips even if you are NOT in a leadership role!):

TIP #1: Practice observing both how you feel, as well as how you react to situations. Keep a diary or a journal that is specific to your emotional intelligence goals. Simply being mindful and having a sense of self-awareness throughout the day can be beneficial to your creative leadership.

TIP #2: Learn to know the difference between responding and reacting. Yes, there IS a difference. When you learn to identify it in others, it will be easier to identify it in yourself.

TIP #3: Study how the pros do it. Make a list of 5 or 10 of the most emotionally intelligent leaders that you can think of. They can be someone you know personally, or someone you've never met; they can be in the same industry as you, or in a completely unrelated field. They might be politicians, activists, celebrities or professional athletes. Watch and study how they leverage emotional intelligence in their successful careers, and take notes.

TIP #4: Stay positive. This can be difficult in some scenarios, but it's never a bad strategy. Take the high road whenever possible (and it's always possible) and get good at keeping things in perspective.

Emotional intelligence isn't necessarily about staying calm, cool and collected in every circumstance (although that may not be a bad idea), but rather staying street-smart, intuitive, and wise in how you interact with others throughout the creative process, and how you can leverage emotion to guide thinking and change the behavior of others in the creative process.

9

The Benefits of Boundaries

A lot of creative personalities don't like boundaries. Many don't like to be told to paint within the lines. While there may be some truth to that, one could also call bullshit on that as well.

Sometimes boundaries can bring out our best work. Sometimes we're limited by budgets, resources, time, or all three. Sometimes we don't realize exactly where the boundaries and limitations are until we're knee deep into a project or close to the finish line.

Lorne Michaels, the creator and producer of Saturday Night Live, says it well, "To me there's no creativity without boundaries. If you're gonna write a sonnet, it's 14 lines, so it's solving the problem within the container.[7]"

Creative people aren't just creative. They are strategists and problem solvers at their core. Where there is a problem that is seeking a solution, there is a creative professional that can make it happen. After all, we've been successfully overcoming boundaries with our creativity since we were children.

Remember playing with Legos® as a kid? There were only a few different types of pieces, in limited colors, and the foundation/floor that you had to work with was only so big. You took what you had to work with, and your creativity and imagination did the rest.

Regardless of what your chosen creative path is in your career – graphic design, songwriting, performing arts, or culinary arts – in a sense, we're all still building with Legos. We only have so many types of pieces available to us, and while many of us pride ourselves as out of the box thinkers, perhaps the opposite is true. Perhaps we are just as effective when we are forced to think *inside* of a box. Often the friction and constraints can light a fire inside us that can produce results that may come across as out of the box thinking, when the opposite is true

Mitch Dowell   45

We can drown in these box" metaphors all day long. But in short, if you're capably-creative enough to think outside of the box, then you should be capably-creative enough to think *inside* the box.

Sometimes there is something as too much freedom in the creative process. Boundaries can often provide us exactly what we need.

10

Understanding Comfort Zones

I don't know many fellow creative professionals who are in comfort zones themselves, or stay in them for very long, and that's a good thing. People who are artistic can often spot comfort in their own work before it becomes a problem. For creative personalities, satisfaction and fulfilment comes through achieving new things, not repeating what has already been done.

However, almost all fellow creatives I know must deal with breaking down and breaking though the comfort zones of others to get their ideas heard, adopted and executed. If you have ever taken a job at an organization that is not known for change, but needs it desperately – and hired you because they finally got around to realizing it - you probably have encountered cultural comfort zones face-to-face, and it was probably anything but comfortable for you.

Sadly, people who are truly stuck in comfort zones will do anything to protect them. Often they are the ones who have been in their current position, or current organization, for a long time. They have gotten used to a certain way of doing things – ways that are no longer successful as they once were, and they have little interest in making modifications even if it is in their best interest.

Where tenure is not much of a factor, age can often be a hidden culprit. The older people get, the worse they tend to get about comfort zones. As we go through life, the more we naturally tend to accumulate "stuff" – marriages, mortgages and moppets – among a host of other life obligations and responsibilities. Therefore, the more we accumulate, the more we have to lose. And the more we have to lose, the fewer risks we tend to take. And the fewer risks we take, the less we are open to trying new ideas by coming out of any comfort zones that may exist.

48   *Designed to Go the Distance*

One significant fact that gets overlooked is that many non-creative professionals who knowingly (or unknowingly) turn down career opportunities – *specifically* to maintain a certain comfort in their careers – fail to realize that true comfort often comes through seizing opportunity. Career creatives commonly tend *NOT* to overlook this.

If your job is to introduce and execute new ideas, your first obligation is to learn to recognize and get uncomfortable with comfort zones that may be in the way of the creative success that is expected of you from those who hire you. And one rude awakening may be realizing that the very people who are expecting that creative success from you may be the very people who are in your way by guarding their comfort zones at all costs.

As a creative professional, you need to pledge allegiance not to the people involved in the process, but to something larger than the people involved. That can be hard to comprehend when it's those people who are paying your invoices and indirectly putting food on your table.

For example, in the bigger picture, a graphic designer is really designing for the target audience, not for the client who is paying for the design work. While the client certainly may not agree with that statement, it's actually the target audience that the design work needs to make the emotional connection with. Using another example, a performing artist needs to make a connection with the ticket-buying concert goers in the theatre, not the booking agency located in another time zone that did the hiring.

For creative professionals, there is always something larger at play. Call it idealism, call it whatever. It is what it is, and it is usually deeply entrenched in the creative soul. This interestingly, and conveniently, serves as a determent to comfort zones for most creatives.

So, the second obligation for the creative professional is to learn how to sell creative ideas to even the laziest and most defensive people and organizations – those who are defending their comfort at all costs – including the cost of your creativity.

If you find that you're working with an organization that is stuck in a comfort zone, or are working with individuals in the creative process who may be, here are a few tips to consider:

TIP #1: Agree on the actual purpose or mission, and on the change that needs to happen, upfront. Many working relationships involving creative professionals fail to sufficiently and thoroughly have this mostly-philosophical conversation upfront. Instead, not seeing eye-to-eye on the creative expectations tends to haunt the projects at hand often *after it's too late* to make the necessary adjustments.

50 *Designed to Go the Distance*

TIP #2: See things from their perspective, but without losing yours. Sometimes within comfort zones exist legitimate reasons for the way things have always been done. But that doesn't mean that they still need to be done that way. Learn as much history and do as much research as you can. Sometimes the comfort zones in question are not just company-deep, but also industry-deep, or influenced by other factors that are external to the project and players involved. See things from other perspectives that may reveal the reality in the creative challenge in front of you, but always come home to your gut perspective as a creative professional. It will rarely lie to you.

TIP #3: Convince them to see what is in it for them. Communicate the business argument for change, rather than solely relying on the creative argument. Discover the language that they truly speak internally, and then sell them on creative change and evolution – in their own language.

TIP #4: Stay positive. Address the issue head-on, but in a non-confrontational way. This may take some artful practice, but it's possible.

In the end, all good ideas demand change. Every highly creative organization knows this. And if you find you're not dealing with one, you have a great opportunity in front of you to be the one creative professional that finally breaks down the wall holding back an organization.

Learn to recognize and get uncomfortable with comfort zones, especially when they are not your own. They do more damage than good for creative professionals.

11

Understanding Burnout

Burnout hurts. It doesn't matter what career field you're in. It hurts both emotionally and physically and can have a ripple effect throughout other areas of your life.

There are many reasons and causes for burnout, and it's important to recognize exactly what the cause is so you can accurately solve the problem. Some common causes of burnout can include a sustained period of intensive creative thinking, a sustained period of heavy workload, or a sustained period of having to lower your standards and deliver mediocre work. Note the word "sustained" in that sentence, as it is an important factor in creative burnout. Let's discuss some of these causes.

Sustained periods of intensive creative thinking can be tricky. As creatives, not only do we love creative thinking, strategic thinking and problem solving – all wrapped up in the same project – we also thrive from the intensity that is involved in the creative process. There is a certain adrenaline rush there that we secretly enjoy. However, over an extended period of deeply intensive creative output, we can start to feel the burn and just need to call a time out. But many of us don't, until it's too late of course.

Sustained periods of heavy workload have similar damaging effects, especially when they involve a fast pace. We can partly blame the advancement of technology for this. We can achieve so much these days in terms of productivity and output, and churn it out 20 times faster than we could a decade or two ago. And of course, higher expectations come along with that - which can also lead to a higher level of expected intensity - the makings of an obvious recipe for burnout.

Burnout can also occur from somewhat of an opposite climate – from being underutilized and exposing yourself to *sustained periods of having to lower your standards* and delivering mediocre work. This is where you can feel like you're in the fast lane with the parking brake on – where you're being held back by the nature of the mediocre work expected from you. And much like a car in drive with the parking brake on, the engine is eventually going to burn out. Humans are no different.

There are some other burnout scenarios to be mindful of. For example, you may love your line of work, but are burned out on the specific industry you're working in. I once knew a graphic designer who worked for a military government contactor. He loved his job, but was just sick of using the same flavor of stock photos in every creative piece. Every photo seemed to either include suits at a meeting table, an army general on a battlefield, or an F-16 in flight. There are certain industries that are just cookie-cutter in terms of their creative, and while creativity is much needed in those environments, you are still expected to draw within the lines. So, while you love what you do and know you're in the right career field, the actual work at hand is just… blah.

In all of these scenarios, there is a common hamster-on-a-wheel feeling. You know it. You feel it. You might even vocalize and complain about it, and vent to others (which I highly recommend, by the way. Don't let burnout eat you up from the inside. Share your struggles with others when and if you can). You know something must change, but for some reason it doesn't, and neither do you. And so, the result is burnout.

The problem with burnout is that it can wear you out, both emotionally and physically to the point where you just don't have the "umph" to make the needed changes.

This reminds me of a story I heard once of a guy who was walking down the road. He heard an awful, horrifying wailing coming from somewhere. As he continued down the road, the sound got closer and closer. It became obvious that someone or something was in a great deal of pain and distress. As he walked by a house, he noticed that there was a dog on the front porch who was wailing, and crying, and whining in a great deal of pain.

The man ran up to the front door and knocked repeatedly with great urgency. Finally, the homeowner answered the door.

The man said, "Sir, your dog here on the front porch appears to be in great pain! He is wailing and crying, and whining and can be heard from blocks away! I'm afraid he might need some immediate veterinary attention!"

The homeowner rolled his eyes, and replied, "Nah. He's just laying on a nail."

The man gasped in surprise, and replied in astonishment, "Well why doesn't he get up off the nail?!?!"

The homeowner replies, "It's not hurting him enough to get off the nail. It's just hurting him enough the cry, moan and wail nonstop."

56   *Designed to Go the Distance*

You can probably see where I'm going with this story. As I mentioned earlier, the problem with burnout is that it can wear you out, both emotionally and physically to the point where you just don't have the "umph" to make the needed changes that you know need to be made. You're lying on an uncomfortable nail in your career, but apparently, it hasn't become uncomfortable enough for you to actually make the needed change.

In some cases, it is possible that other players involved can help you get out of your creative burnout rut. For example, your superiors might be able to change up the nature of your projects, or your clients may be willing to work and interact with you on projects in a different way that can alleviate some of the "blah", but this may only work in some cases.

Regardless of the specific situation, you must find your "umph" again and put it into motion in a way that will lead to the career fulfillment you envision. Don't expect others to do the work for you. They may be able to help, but much of the "umph" needs to come from you. After all, you're the one suffering the burnout.

While much of this chapter deals with creative burnout that has already taken place, how do you prevent burnout in the first place? Prevention is not always possible, sometimes burnout just happens in creative careers, but here are a few prevention tips to consider.

Mitch Dowell   57

TIP 1: Perform your work with a sense of purpose. Most creatives are hired not just to create, but to solve problems. Try to get fascinated again with the problem at hand. Perhaps the real problem doesn't lie with the problem that needs to be solved, but with the fact that you're churning out the *same solutions to the problem*. Perhaps it's not the problem that has become mundane, but your creative output actually has. Take a step back and see if that indeed might be a contributor to your burnout.

TIP 2: Get good at seeing things coming. Don't just look as far as the hood of the car, get good at seeing things coming down the road. This can help prevent burnout that is specifically associated with work overload. The quicker you can see potential overload starting to take shape, the quicker you can delegate work as needed, or address the overload issue before it arrives and becomes disruptive.

TIP 3: Get better at just saying "no" to certain things. Creatives don't often like to pass up on opportunities. We are ambitious at heart - even the most introverted creatives among us. But as we go through our careers, we need to get better at saying "yes" to projects and jobs that are *in our creative-best-interest*, and sometimes that means also getting better at saying "no" to those that aren't – and learning to intuitively know the difference.

There are many other tips that I can suggest to prevent creative burnout – specifically to where one's health and well-being might play a factor. But since I discuss some of those topics elsewhere in this book, I've just leave you with the tips above.

Creative burnout. It's not an uncommon thing with creative professionals. But it doesn't have to do us in.

12

Balancing Career and Life

I'm the last person on the planet to be giving advice about work/life balance. I have successfully failed miserably in that department. Creativity is not something that you can easily turn on and off like a light switch. Therefore, some of us are always on. While my client work is currently done for the week and I am technically off the clock, here I am at 4:32AM on a Sunday morning typing this very sentence.

Yes, it's true. Creatives never stop creating. It's both a blessing and a curse. But in the long run, that reality is not sustainable in the bigger life picture – that is if you want to have a meaningful life outside of your work, and I'll assume that most people do.

As I mentioned in the introduction of this book, I come primarily from a graphic design and visual branding background. An interesting observation that I have noticed about the graphic design career field specifically, is that there seems to be very few first-career graphic designers over the age of 45 (second and third-career crossover designers are a different story).

So, where do all those first-career designers go? What is the cause for such a drop-off? Do they eventually burn out creatively? Does the career field max out on earning potential? Do other life obligations make it harder to compete with younger creative talent that have more time to commit to the field? The answer could lie in any or a combination of those possibilities.

One thing is for sure. As we go through life, we naturally build and piece together our more complete life story outside of our careers. Chances are that we won't be living the same kind of life in our 40s that we were living in our 20s. Over time we might accumulate marriages, mortgages, and moppets. We have long-term relationships to maintain, mouths at home to feed, and college tuitions to save up for. Or if we don't end up building a family, we

62   *Designed to Go the Distance*

still have hobbies and personal goals that will need to be nurtured outside of our careers according to what we want our overall life picture to look like.

[Sigh]. So here is what we all need to go do...

Paint a picture of what your perfect life would look like, not just career-wise but overall - and then go out and create it. Understand that the different areas of your life can not only co-exist with each other, but also benefit each other. It's your life, it can be anything you want it to be. You call the shots.

Although that advice sounds simple, most of us rarely go out and do that. We're either too busy to slow down enough to re-focus, or we fall into the "busy-trap" in the process of trying to paint that perfect picture. Simply put, our society sucks at work/life balance. We just do.

Doing a simple web search for work/life balance techniques will reveal many of the usual no-brainer tips – ya know, the ones that most of us have failed to fully apply to our own lives. But for the career creatives who are actually reading this book, there are a few common time-and-life-sucking sources out there that tend to do us in, and here are some tips to help manage them...

TIP #1: Identify specific clients or specific processes that are sucking up all your time. Chances are that it is not WHAT you do for a living that is sucking all your time up, but WHO you're working for, and perhaps HOW you're working with them.

TIP #2: Choose the right employer or clients in the first place. Sometimes we get lured into the attraction of the project, and fail to pay attention as to whether the type of client or employer is actually in our best interest.

TIP #3: Learn how to say "no." Most all creatives suck at this. We're in the business of tearing down boundaries and pushing the envelope. Often that means saying "yes" to more things than perhaps we should. Learn what you need to say "no" to, and feel confident in doing so. It can be empowering.

TIP #4: Minimize distractions. Sometimes we suck at time management because we allow ourselves to get distracted. Knock it off. Throw on the headphones, turn off the smartphone, turn off the phone lines – do whatever it takes to get lost in your work and to stay there for as long as possible

So there you have it – a few work/life balance tips from a total knucklehead when it comes to actual work/life balance. "Do as I say, not as I do." You will thank yourself someday.

13

Handling Criticism Like a Pro

While creative professionals are very emotional creatures by nature, and while regular criticism and rejection just goes with the territory of any creative career, it can still be an ongoing challenge that can take its toll over time. The trick is to separate yourself from the actual criticism.

Forming a "tough skin" when it comes to handling criticism and rejection is one approach. But perhaps forming a "smart skin" might be a better way to think about it.

There is value in criticism - that is if you're smart enough, and willing enough to look for it. That does not mean that you should adopt any and all feedback that comes your way. You know better than that. Use your street-smarts, keep the good and ignore the bad.

The first thing you should do is chill out and reserve immediate emotion and consider the source of the criticism. Is it coming from someone you respect and trust? If so, there can be value in the feedback. That doesn't mean that they are right, but if in your gut you respect and trust this person, value their feedback accordingly.

Also, sometimes what people say is not what they actually mean. The more criticism you receive in your career, the better you will get at identifying exactly what people are trying to communicate.

Sometimes people are just having a bad day. Something minor becomes major to them, but in the end, it isn't that important. Therefore, it's important to get good at identifying the emotion associated with the delivery of the criticism. Not just the tone of voice, but if the criticism is delivered in-person, pay attention to body language and the vibe in the room. The objective here is to separate the delivery of the criticism from the necessary details that you will need to access the value of the criticism.

Sometimes it's ideal to have a more in-depth discussion about the criticism and this may require you to open up in front of your client about your overall process, and your way of thinking. While this

66   *Designed to Go the Distance*

may be helpful to the client to reach a needed level of understanding, you want to make sure that you don't open up too much to the point of making yourself vulnerable in front of a client. If you give an inch and they take you a mile, they will take you for a ride every single time, because now they know that they can. Be careful there.

If you're on the introverted side of the personality scale, then chances are that you're a professional "internalizer." If you're a pro at internalizing criticism, and you're going to do it anyway, that's OK. But put a deadline on it. Decide when to move on. Internalizing criticism for too long can have long-lasting, damaging effects that will sneak up on you throughout your career.

The most important thing that you can do in regards to this topic is to thank people for their criticism, regardless of the situation. It's the right, human thing to do. They are taking the time and injecting some risk into the business relationship by offering their criticism, and they may be just as uncomfortable giving criticism as you may feel receiving it.

One last note about receiving criticism. Everything I've said to this point is considering that the person you're dealing with is someone you are OK dealing with in general. Every now and then you will come to the realization that you have a total asshole on your hands. It's a gut feeling and a moment of truth that you will value like no other. Start strategizing your escape plan to possibly fire the client, or to move on to another employment or working situation. But until you're actually able to do that, use some of the tips earlier on in this chapter to the best of your abilities to work your way through the project at hand.

There are assholes in the world. You're not stupid, you know one when you see one. Even in the most stressful situations, try to kill people with kindness. But don't lie down like a rug either. Take the high road until it intersects with a better road.

Embrace criticism, rejection and failure. It just goes with the territory of bringing your creativity to the world that needs it. It can be of immense value if you recognize where your art might actually need it.

14

When Side Projects Just Make Sense

Sometimes creative professionals need to get away, without actually "getting away." This is where the value of an occasional, or regular side project comes into play.

There are many common reasons why creative professionals feel the need to "get away." Perhaps you've reached a level of temporary boredom in your job, but the job is still worth keeping for various reasons. Or perhaps you're bored with the people you work with and you feel the need to network outside of your usual tribe. Or perhaps you just have a creative itch that needs to be scratched that the day gig can't help you reach.

There can be numerous, valid reasons why it would be beneficial to consider doing some work on the side, rather than throwing in the towel on the main gig altogether. You might just need a little something that can accent the main gig – and that can perhaps allow you to rediscover your passion for day job.

Compared to many other career fields, there is rarely a shortage of side work out there for the average creative professional (sometimes it can be easier to find side work than full-time work!), and this can add to the allure of it all.

However, there are a few things that you should consider before taking on side work.

First, if you work a full-time gig, chances are that any side projects you take on will involve evening or weekend hours, cutting into the rest of your life. So, it's important to choose your side projects wisely and make sure that you have as much control over the project as possible, right down to scope of project and the deadlines involved. So, let your *side gig* know that it is NOT your *main gig*, and be open about your intentions before performing any work.

Side projects should always be low-pressure and low risk. They should be fun, yet force you to think in different ways. They should either be a way to learn new things, or an opportunity to brush up on your current weaknesses.

Secondly, make sure you're legally in the clear to do side work in regards to any agreements you may have signed or are obligated to with the main employer. Things could get messy otherwise. And it's always a good idea to add an extra layer of common sense regarding any potential conflicts of interest. Put yourself in your employer's shoes and try to see things from their perspective.

And speaking of that main employer, even if you're legally in the clear to do side work, there are some employers out there who may not appreciate their employees doing the same kind of work on the side. You may have to deal with some potential insecurities there and the relationship may start to get weird.

While you may never have "sold your soul at the crossroads" with them, legally or otherwise, some employers may try to read between the lines and assume you are looking for greener pastures. They may suddenly feel the need to compete with your side work by adding more work to your plate or keeping you late more often. And if you come in one morning a bit more groggy or tired than usual, then you can bet you will get the third degree about it, in true passive aggressive form. In other words, they become the bitchy girlfriend or boyfriend who feels shafted by your newfound side interest.

To avoid that scenario, you should honestly assess the relationships you have at your main gig and decide whether it even makes sense to inform them of your side activities at all. If you're legally in the clear, then sometimes it's best to just keep what you do on the side to yourself.

But if the timing and project scope is right, then the benefits of an occasional or regular side gig can accent your creative career in many positive ways.

15

Depression and The Creative Pro

This is a pretty heavy duty topic that should not be taken lightly. I am in no position whatsoever to discuss this topic with any remote hint of authority or clinical expertise. The topic of depression and creativity is very widely studied and researched from those in positions of proper authority to do so. Just do a simple news search on the web and you will find plenty of research with minimal clicking.

I've worked with a fair share of creative professionals who have suffered from bouts of depression, and I have experienced, first-hand, the many career field-specific challenges that can unfortunately lead to it. After all, the need to discuss many of those challenges is why I wrote this book. So, I'm going to chime in on this topic from a creative professional's perspective, but that is all it is – one man's unauthoritative opinion.

First off, let's get one thing straight – depression is more widespread than most of us might think, as many cases will go undiagnosed. All humans are emotional creatures who accumulate life experiences that range from pure joy to pure hell. Throw in biological issues like chemical imbalances and genetics, and one could indeed face many uphill battles in both life and career.

Specially regarding creativity, there are many household names in creative career fields who have struggled with the disease. Some well-known names from history include Ludwig van Beethoven, Vincent van Gogh, Georgia O'Keeffe and Charles Schulz[8]. More modern day names include Ellen DeGeneres, Demi Lovato, Ashley Judd, Adam Duritz, Billy Joel, Sheryl Crow and many others[9] [10].

If you're a creative professional (or anyone for that matter) and feel that you're in a funk that you just can't seem to shake, start off by visiting your primary care physician as soon as possible. They can often be the perfect entry point to identifying the proper treatment that is right for you. Your need for a straightjacket and a rubber room is most likely quite slim. A combination of lifestyle change and proper medication can often do the trick. I don't have authority or expertise to elaborate on the medicinal portion, but I'll share my thoughts on the lifestyle bit.

"Exercise and socialize" is always good advice, regardless of what your funk-level is. Something as simple as going for a regular walk or a jog can help. All you need is your favorite pair of sneakers and a good pair of headphones with your favorite tunes or audiobook, and away you go. So many sporting activities these days seem to require a crapload of gear, and that can kill the mood of simple exercise. *Don't overthink things.* Just get your blood flow going and your heart rate up a tad. And although indoor treadmills and exercise bikes will work, if fresh air is an option, get outside for your exercise as much as possible.

The other part is socializing. If you're a creative personality on the introverted side of the personality scale, socializing can be excruciating and agonizing even on your best days. Throw in depression as a possible factor in the mix, and yeah right, you're not leaving the house, are you?

But let's think about that for a moment. The list of celebrities listed earlier in this chapter - the list of household names of creative professionals that includes famous actors, musicians, and artists – if you are indeed suffering from depression, you're in good company. Sometimes just knowing that someone else might be going through what you're going through can provide some temporary relief. But unless you've got some awesome connections, it might not be possible to just pick up the phone and call some of those famous names and share your experiences. Start with your immediate creative circle. Call up someone you know in your career field and get together for coffee. Even if you don't feel up to sharing about the funk you're in, sometimes just getting together with someone else from your "tribe" can be helpful. But I encourage you to consider taking a chance, and opening up with them somehow, someway. If they are a fellow creative professional, chances are they may not just understand what you could be going through, but they have gone through it themselves, but just haven't revealed it to anyone.

Only *you* can exercise and socialize - that is 100% in your control. But if there is a chemical imbalance going on under the surface (and you can't self-diagnose that), go see a doctor. Just like you take your car to a mechanic if you hear a weird noise or an unfamiliar vibration while driving, you have an obligation to do the same with your body, mind and soul. Just do it.

One last thing to discuss on this topic - because one might consider it as a remedy for possible depression - is avoiding any overindulgence in alcohol and drugs. Much like I provided a sample list of famous, household names with depression earlier in this chapter, I can also rattle off a list of famous, creative, household names who are no longer living as a result of overindulgence in alcohol and drugs (perhaps as an attempted masking for depression). I'm sure you can rattle off a similar list, too. So let's not have to go there by keeping an eye on what we put in our bodies, and being sensible about our diet.

So, if you're in a funk that you feel has a hold on you, go see your primary care doctor and chat about it. While they may not be specialized in such matters, they can refer you to the right medical professionals if they feel you do indeed need a referral. It's all about taking that FIRST step. It could be the best step you ever take in your life.

On the other hand, if you're NOT in a funk and don't feel that this chapter applies to you at this time - awesome! But keep an eye on things as you go through your creative career. As mentioned earlier in this chapter, the topic of depression and creativity is very widely studied and researched and it's important to keep oneself in good health as we offer our creative talents to the world as a profession.

16

The Final Word: Paying it Forward

The creative professional lifestyle is one that has been widely studied and researched, and new perspectives are always being published, tested and argued. No two creatives manage and navigate through professional experiences the same way.

The topics covered in this book are some examples of the perfect, never-ending conversations that are out there. And since they are never-ending discussions, there is no "perfect" way to close out this kind of book (or at least this First Edition, anyway). So, I would like to do so instead by kindly asking a favor – for you to "pay it forward" in your creative career as much as your time allows.

The concept of paying it forward is not about repaying a favor to the original person who did the favor, but to do a good deed in the future for someone else instead.

Perhaps you've heard stories of people at the drive-thru of a coffee shop paying for the person's order in the car behind them. That is a simple example of paying it forward.

Writing this book, in a sense, is an attempt at paying it forward for me. I'm hoping to share some career experiences and tips with readers that can help them in their own creative professional journeys.

Share your knowledge, stories, experiences and intuition unselfishly with not only other creatives, but with non-creatives as well. They need to hear it. They need to know what it takes to be a creative professional and what hardships and sacrifices are involved, not just at the project level, but also down to the lifestyle level.

Mentor someone. It will not just be good for them, but good for you, too. Mentoring is a two-way street. Learning goes both ways. It doesn't matter how old you are, how long you've been doing what you've been doing, what your job title is, how many awards you've won or haven't won. We never stop learning, and therefore should never stop teaching and mentoring.

Be there when another creative professional needs you to be there. And I'm not just talking at the project level, I'm also talking about lending an ear and providing words of wisdom when needed. As I suggested in the Introduction of this book, think of this book more as a late-night barstool or coffeehouse conversation between two creatives. A creative pep talk so-to-speak. Creatives need that, ya know. Keep that barstool warm or that coffeepot full. Lean on each other when needed – build relationships. We all possess a certain creative magic within us that can change the world, even in the smallest of ways. We have an obligation to it, and a responsibility for it. But it can take its toll. So BE THERE for other creatives.

Paying it forward is just good common sense, and it can help others create a career that is *designed to go the distance.*

About the Author

Photo Credit: Katie Baroody

Mitch Dowell is the Founder & Creative Director of Branding Experiences, a marketing, branding and design company in the Baltimore/DC metro area and has been involved in visual branding, graphic design and creative marketing for over 20 years.

Mitch has worked on both the corporate and agency sides of the fence and has spent much of his career in the trenches doing hands-on design and creative work himself. With this first-hand experience, together with having managed other creative professionals – both in-house as well as outsourced talent – Mitch has accumulated a wealth of experiences over the years that have been the basis for this book.

Mitch is often sought out by mainstream and business media for his expertise on the topics of marketing, branding and design, and is frequently booked for speaking engagements on similar topics. You can learn more about Mitch at www.mitchdowell.com.

NOTES

NOTES

NOTES

NOTES

NOTES

NOTES

NOTES

Index

A

ad agencies 15
Adam Duritz, ... 84
Albert Einstein 7
alcohol and drugs 87
Amelia Earhart 42
Art Director 39
Ashley Judd 84
authors 12

B

Billy Joel 85
Bob Dylan 7
Burnout 61

C

cartoons, ... 28
Charles Schulz 84
chef 20
chemical imbalances 84
comfort zones 44, 47, 54, 55, 56, 57, 58, 59
computer programmers 15
Corporate America 16
corporate environments 15
creative (definition) 6
Creative Director 39

criticism
criticism 21, 75, 76, 77, 78
crossover designers 70

D

Demi Lovato 84
depression 83

E

Ellen DeGeneres 84
emotional intelligence (definition) 45
Exercise 85
extrovert 11

G

George Carlin 42
George Lucas 29
Georgia O'Keeffe 84
graphic design 2, 14, 38, 70, 92
graphic design culture 38
graphic designers 12, 15
gut feeling 78

H

Henry Ford 7, 42, 43

I

idealism 57
Imaginative (definition)...................6
in-house creatives...........................15
introvert 11
intuition 21

J

John Lennon 29

L

Leadership styles 16
Lego 52
long-term relationships 71
Lorne Michaels................................52
Ludwig van Beethoven...................84

M

Martin Luther King Jr,...................42
Mentoring 90
Meryl Steep.......................................5
Michael Jackson 7
military government contactor......63

N

National Football League...............34

O

non-conformist..............................41

O

orchestra conductor 14
originality...14
Originality (definition)....................6

P

Papa Smurf.......................................48
paying it forward.............................90
personal health................................26
personal relationships....................26
post-creative risk 21
Prince...7
Princess Diana,................................42
problem solving 13

R

rejection 75, 78
Risk. 19
Robin Williams..................................7
Rocky..8
Rosa Parks..42
runner's high 26

S

Saturday Night Live 52
sense of purpose..............................66

Mitch Dowell   91

Sheryl Crow 85
side project 80
socializing 86
solitude 13
songwriter 14
Songwriting 13
status quo 46, 47
Steve Jobs 7, 42, 43
strategic thinking 13

T

The Beatles 13
the creative divide 39
Thomas Edison 7, 42
Tony Robbins 16
tribal behavior 38

U

unscheduled ideas 26

V

Vincent van Gogh 84
visual branding 2, 70, 92

W

Woody Allen 7
work/life balance 28, 29, 31, 69, 71, 72
workaholics 26

Y

yin and yang 40
Yoda 48

References

[1] Meryl Streep Quotes
http://www.azquotes.com/author/14233-Meryl_Streep

[2] Creative (definition):
http://www.dictionary.com/browse/creative

[3] Expression (definition): http://www.dictionary.com/browse/expression

[4] Imagination (definition): http://www.dictionary.com/browse/imagination

[5] Pro Football Hall of Fame, From Number 1 to the Hall of Fame,
http://www.profootballhof.com/football-history/no-1-to-the-hall-of-fame/

[6] Emotional Intelligence (definition)
https://en.wikipedia.org/wiki/Emotional_intelligence

[7] Lorne Michaels on Boundaries,
https://www.brainyquote.com/quotes/quotes/l/lornemicha501975.html

[8] 8 Artists Who Suffered from Mental Illness,
http://www.mnn.com/lifestyle/arts-culture/stories/8-artists-who-suffered-mental-illness

[9] 27 Celebrities on Dealing with Depression and Bipolar Disorder
https://www.buzzfeed.com/juliapugachevsky/celebrities-on-dealing-with-depression-and-bipolar-disord?utm_term=.eszBwmWL6#.msBqD95BK

[10] 43 Inspiring Celebs Who Lived with Depression
http://www.huffingtonpost.com/2011/08/31/celebs-with-depression_n_942771.html

REGARDLESS OF WHERE YOU PURCHASED THIS BOOK, PLEASE CONSIDER VISITING YOUR FAVORITE ONLINE BOOK RETAILER AND LEAVING A REVIEW. YOUR THOUGHTS ARE VALUED AND APPRECIATED.

Made in the USA
Lexington, KY
04 January 2017